Who Says Men Don't Care? A Man's Guide to Balanced and Guilt-Free Caregiving

by James V. Gambone, Ph.D.
and
Rhonda W. Travland, M.S.

**Foreword by Gary Barg
Founder and Editor-in-Chief of
Today's Caregiver Magazine and
Caregiver.com**

Who Says Men Don't Care?
A Man's Guide to Balanced and Guilt-Free Caregiving

By James V. Gambone, Ph.D. and
Rhonda W. Travland, M.S.

Foreword by Gary Barg, Founder and Editor-in-Chief of
Today's Caregiver Magazine and Caregiver.com

Interior design by Wendy J. Johnson, Elder Eye Design, www.ElderEye.com

ISBN:1460906888
ISBN-13: 978-1460906880

www.MaleGuideForCaregiving.com

Acknowledgements

We want to acknowledge the people who helped us with this guide. First, the caregivers who acted as early readers and constructive critics: Vince Marolla, Steve Coleman, Dan Dailey, Chuck Denny, Kristine Dwyer, Gary Mansfield, Connie Kyle, and Andrea Stevens.

We would also like to recognize our respective spouses, Wendy J. Johnson and David A. Travland, Ph.D., for their ongoing support throughout this project; Dave for the many hours of work he put into helping us get this Guide ready for publication; and Wendy for her Elder Eye interior design and cover design consultation.

———

Contents

———

Foreword
by Gary Edward Barg

Fred strode up to the registration table at our third annual Philadelphia Fearless Caregiver Conference, red-faced and looking like he wanted to punch something or someone, and the sooner the better. "I am a caregiver for my wife who is living with Alzheimer's disease, and her doctor told me I needed to come to this event," he blurted out as he walked into the session room to find a seat. The first events of the day are always the morning question and answer sessions, which are designed to allow family caregivers the opportunity to ask questions of caregiving experts, share their own stories, and interact with one another.

After about an hour of male and female family caregivers laughing, sharing, and even crying at times, Fred, still red-faced, raised his hand and motioned for me to come over with the handheld microphone I had been bringing to caregivers who expressed a desire to talk. Oh, well, I thought, time to get punched. I soon realized that the reason for Fred's red face had changed and now he was actually crying. For the first time since his caregiving began, Fred realized that he was not alone as a family caregiver. And, in fact, he had found himself sitting in the middle of a room filled with kindred souls.

Fred is not alone—not by a long shot. The National Alliance for Caregiving reported that there are 65.7 million family caregivers in the nation and of them, 34 percent are male caregivers. Yet, even though a full third of the United States' population is caregiving for loved ones, as the old saying goes, *Once you've seen one caregiving family, you've seen one caregiving family.* There can be as many similarities among caregivers as there are differences, past the point that we all, male or female, are involved with our own labors of love.

As a male caregiver, I understood Fred's challenges as well as I do Hal's, although their situations are significantly different. Hal faced the fear of crossing the Rubicon that so many male caregivers must face at some point or another—changing his mother's adult undergarments. In my role as editor-in-chief of *Today's Caregiver* magazine, I have written about many men who are taking on the role of family caregiver for loved ones. Along with Fred and Hal, there is Terry, a long-distance caregiver who organized his mother's care as well as any four-star general would organize his forces to wage a successful battle. And then there is Mark, who is a hands-on partner with his wife Cheryl as they care for Cheryl's mom. Mark has taken it upon himself to become what I like to call a caregiver's caregiver; supporting Cheryl as a full partner in care, but also making sure that Cheryl is cared for as well.

These stories from male family caregivers and many more are why I am so very honored to be able to write this foreword for *Who Says Men Don't Care? A Man's Guide to Balanced and Guilt-Free Caregiving.* Dr. James Gambone and Rhoda Travland have written a Guide that creates a clear, thoughtful, and extremely readable overview of the lives of male caregivers. I am never one to stereotype any caregiver, male or female; but like the authors, I believe that all of us bring our own history and personal characteristics to everything we do for our loved ones. As our caregiving challenges begin, it is extremely important to understand how our character types can help to influence our responses to family caregiving. This book offers a place to start such an analysis. The CARES Assessment is designed to help you decide which characteristic type you fall under, including Lone Wolf, Manager, Worker, Perfectionist, and Techno-Virtual caregiver.

As the book states: *Men are reputed to be more logical than women, and more in control of their emotions.* There is not much truth in this stereotype. I wholeheartedly agree, and I have seen as many "types" of caregivers as it is possible to imagine—men who are extremely emotional, women who are managerial in nature. The truth remains that although there can be no stereotypes, as in all things to do with human beings, past can be prologue when it comes to how we will respond to external stimulus.

Male caregivers can, at times, feel like fish out of water when dealing with the daily challenges of family caregiving. *With Who Says Men Don't Care? A Man's Guide to Balanced and Guilt-Free Caregiving,* they can finally understand the waters in which they find themselves swimming as family caregivers.

– Gary Edward Barg

Founder and Editor-in-Chief of *Today's Caregiver* magazine and www.caregiver.com, author of *The Fearless Caregiver,* and host to more than a hundred Fearless Caregiver conferences

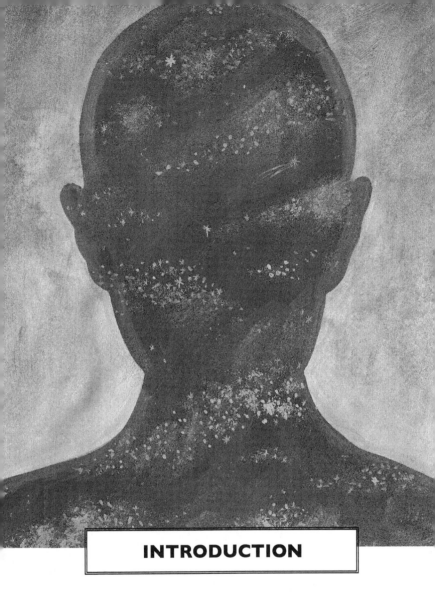

INTRODUCTION

Our hunch is that you picked up this Guide because you are a guy, and you have been pressed into service helping someone close to you. You may not have given it much thought. Someone needed your help and you were close by.

You may not know this, but there are millions of men out there doing exactly what you are doing. Caregiving is usually a role that begins out of authentic love and a simple desire to do the right thing.

You are probably already aware that caring for someone is not always easy. Sacrifices are involved, and the path is filled with questions and obstacles.

We also know that many of you may not even think of yourselves as "caregivers." You are husbands, sons, fathers, grandfathers, or just friends caring for someone you love. Where you find yourself right now may be a matter of circumstance, or an emergency—and nobody gave you a title. We will use the simplest meaning of *caregiver* in this Guide: someone who is paying close attention and gives care to someone else.

What you may not know is that there is a lot of knowledge available about caring for others. This knowledge can help you stay upbeat, healthy, and balanced. Our job is to bring you this knowledge in a form you can use.

This year in the United States alone, more than 22 million men—just like you—will care for a chronically ill, disabled, or aged family member or friend. There are a lot of people in situations similar to yours, but only one pair of feet in *your* shoes.

Sometimes being a caregiver can be a pretty lonely and demoralizing place. We know that when you become a caregiver your world suddenly shrinks, and in this smaller world, little problems or issues can become much larger.

Chances are, you are dealing with much more than someone's physical and health-care needs alone. When a person we love needs long- or short-term care, what they and we value most—our dignity, independence, family relationships, our property, even our life savings— becomes fragile overnight. Everything that has provided the foundation of that person's life—and maybe yours—is suddenly at risk.

Your role is therefore more than just that of an unpaid nurse or aide; chances are you are at once a guardian and defender, confidant and counselor, companion and entertainer, cook and dishwasher, housekeeper and repairman, bookkeeper and planner, manager and magician, gofer and general troubleshooter. In its own way, this is likely the most demanding role you have ever embraced in your whole life.

Everything depends on your approach, persistence, dedication, versatility, and endurance—and yet almost no one ever notices or thinks about you or your needs. You are a forgotten man. You are on your own.

It is natural enough that the person you are caring for, for better or worse (and for richer and poorer!), is the star of the drama you are living out, and it is unlikely that anything will change this. You are a supporting actor and as such, you must see to your own needs and welfare. No one else will.

———

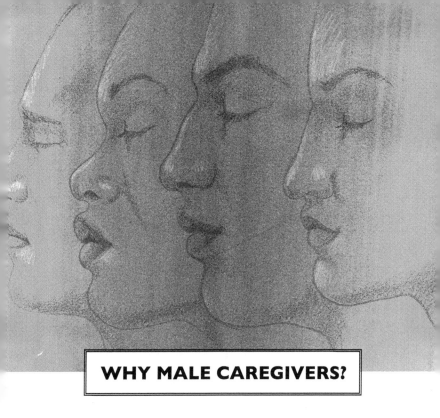

WHY MALE CAREGIVERS?

Ten years ago only 25 percent of caregivers were men, but with the sweeping demographic and social changes that are changing the face of America, today in excess of 36–40 percent of caregivers are male, and this proportion will continue to rise.

Caregiving is becoming an equal-opportunity responsibility.

Yet we all know men and women are different. They are wired differently, and as a result they approach life challenges in different ways. The professional literature about caregiving has not yet caught up with the significant demographic shift and has not considered the unique perspectives and needs of men who care—that is, until now.

Yes, male caregivers are really different than women.*

Men as Caregivers...	Women as Caregivers...
Typically seek outcomes regardless of process	Seek peace first, then worry about the process
Don't care about why there is a problem, just want to fix it	Want to know why before they can make a change
Want instant results with interventions	Are more patient with the process of care and recovery
See obstacles as a challenge, a setback, or personal failure	See obstacles as normal and adjust with the challenges
Value self-reliance	Value collaboration
Tend to be direct in communications	Tend to soften the tough messages

We do not claim these differences are representative of all men and women and we categorically say neither gender is inherently superior; we simply say they are different and present unique challenges and exhibit different gender-based strengths for the caregiver.

———

HOW CAN THIS GUIDE HELP?

This Guide will not attempt to train you about how to improve care delivery techniques; there are plenty of training resources for caregivers already out there. The *Appendix* at the end of this Guide will help you choose the resource most appropriate for your situation.

Instead, we focus on helping you understand your caregiving "style," satisfy your most important needs and motivations, and stay healthy and balanced while providing effective care. In other words, how you can keep growing and improving while acting unselfishly.

Selflessness is an admirable trait, but if it is not counter-balanced by self-interest, it will transform you into a martyr and, as we all know, martyrs are by definition not survivors. Martyrdom only works if you are dead. Caregiving can wear down the strongest of men. It requires a tremendous expenditure of physical, psychological, and emotional energy.

If you drain a battery without recharging it, it dies. We will show you how to recharge yourself and to focus and practice *self-determination* in your caregiving. This means actively and intentionally making personal life decisions, knowing your strengths and weaknesses, and choosing from real alternatives when it comes to your involvement in all aspects of health treatment, planning, and the organization of any service you provide. Self-determination also means having as *balanced and guilt-free* a caregiving lifestyle as possible. This powerful combination will charge your battery and keep it vital and powerful enough to get you through whatever ordeal you may be facing as your loved one's "main man" and caregiver.

This Guide will also show you how to tap this power source in ethical, creative, and effective ways. It will enable you to look back on your caregiving experiences with pride and enduring satisfaction and with as little guilt or regret as is humanly possible.

David was caring for his wife Cheryl who had terminal ovarian cancer. He told us that the most important lesson he learned in his caregiving experience was to focus on being creative. He tried to find the best in even the worst situation. Creativity was in his words a "preoccupation" that enabled him and his wife to try to make the best out of the absolute worst. It was a way of making their remaining time together as rewarding as humanly possible.

This story from his care-taking experience shows the potential of how to find meaning and be a creative male caregiver. When it came time to plan the funeral, they decided that instead of paying for the usual casket, they would offer a local artist a chance to design a casket for them. This happened near the end of the illness, when the caregiving tasks and the pain were at their most challenging. David said that while doing this did not change their suffering, it did give them something else to focus on and made it more meaningful.

We sincerely hope you will find creative ways to use this Guide and that you'll look at caregiving differently when you are finished.

So, What's The Drill?

If you think of caregiving as you might think about a major business, military or disaster relief operation, there· are certain logical steps you would take to make sure everything runs smoothly. For example, you need to think about the assets you have in place, what additional resources you might need, the quality of your supply lines, and the timing of any necessary strategic retreat from your current position.

We offer you some simple tools to help you prepare for even the most tortuous and confounding personal experiences that caregiving can bring. We know you are probably already experiencing new burdens on your time, energy, and resources; we do not want to add to the problems. This book can help you lay out a good strategy, hopefully ease some of your burdens, and reduce your chances of feeling anger, resentment, or burnout.

Getting Started

We begin by asking you to focus on your personal assets and liabilities. No, we will not ask you to "get in touch with your feelings" but we will tell you that most if not *all* of the answers to any caregiving dilemma you face are already inside you. By examining your motivations for becoming a caregiver in the first place, you can then determine what additional help you may need. The Guide will help you establish your personal priorities with confidence.

The short assessment exercises and personal caregiving stories will help you sort out relevant strengths, weaknesses, and opportunities and create realistic goals. They will also help you distinguish between the myths and realities of caregiving and help you choose from *real* alternatives that place *you* at the center of all aspects of health treatment, planning, and the organization of services you or others will provide.

Even if you are deeply involved in a caregiving situation right now—especially one that is not going particularly well—it is not too late to make changes. You can make mid- and even late-course corrections for your own well-being as well as for the well-being and benefit of the person for whom you are caring.

The next step simply is to read on. One paragraph at a time—one day at a time—your journey can get better, whatever the shape of your present crisis.

The *self-determined male caregiver* is a man who is willing to look honestly at who he really is. When it comes right down to it, the most important person in any caregiving situation is you. Without you, the person you love would likely be worse off.

The real key to using the Guide successfully will therefore be your own honesty. If you are being honest with yourself, you will be able to be honest with the person for whom you are caring. Here is a quick tool you can use to assess your strengths and weaknesses and your particular caregiving style.

―――

The CARES Assessment™ stands for the traits that help determine your individual behavior (inspired by the Five Factor Model of Personality). Taking the assessment simply allows you to select where you perceive yourself on a scale of caregiving strengths and weaknesses.

Definitions of "CARES"

C = Conscientiousness – meaning seriousness of purpose and dedication to results.

A = Agreeableness – meaning a willingness to be influenced by others versus confrontational tendencies.

R = Responsiveness – meaning how tuned in one is to his or her immediate environment and how influenced or reactive to external events.

E = Extraversion – meaning how comfortable one is with noise, distraction, and social stimulation (i.e., how sociable).

S = Sensitivity – meaning an affinity for new ideas, methods, and philosophies.

Keep in mind that there is no right or wrong answer in this assessment. This is not a scientific exercise. It is only intended to get you thinking about yourself as a male caregiver.

Try to evaluate yourself in the mindset of your pre-caregiver days. You have made adjustments in your new role and now you need to look back at who you were. While we know you can never go back in time and be what you once were, you can recapture important aspects of your life and understand that you have options.

Instructions: Read through the CARES Assessment. Pick one or two characteristics that best fit you in each CARES row and circle the number next to it. When you've finished circling the numbers, add up the numbers in each row and put your total in the column on the right. Then add up those total numbers as a cumulative total and put that number in the box at the bottom right. You can now match your total numerical score to one (or more) of the Caregiver Types and read the description for your type.

We realize there are no perfect "types" of caregivers. Read the descriptions for all of the Caregiver Types. You will probably see parts of yourself in each, but typically only one or two will dominate.

THE CARES ASSESSMENT™

	1	2	3	4	5	Totals
Conscientiousness	Feels unprepared, a procrastinator, distractible, impulsive, poorly organized	Fragile confidence, casual about obligations, quits difficult tasks, disorganized, makes hasty decisions	Sets achievable goals, balances work & play, organized where necessary, usually confident, moderately high self-esteem	Normally prepared and confident, reliable, puts work before play, productive & disciplined	Industrious, disciplined, highly confident, competitive, cautious about decisions	
Agreeableness	Cynical, skeptical, tough minded, blunt, can be combative and unsympathetic, positive self-image, wants to win	Slow to trust others, trouble compromising, seeks praise, proud of own achievements, can be insensitive, not humble	Tactful, trusting with evidence, willing to help if really needed, a negotiator, can keep ego in check, seeks win-win outcomes	Readily trusts others, a team player, yields to others in a conflict, modest, reluctant to take credit, helpful to others	Humble, self-effacing, passive, puts others' needs above own, easily manipulated, prefers to follow, not lead	
Responsiveness	Expressive, can be anxious, a worrier, reacts to small provocations, may panic, depends on approval from others	Concerned, easily provoked, sensitive, slow recovery	Can be provoked, recovers well from setbacks, deliberate, pays attention to external and internal signals	Even tempered, rational under pressure, persistent	Unflappable, cool head, deliberate, controlled, guilt free, cheerful, powerful internal guidance	
Extraversion	Reserved, a loner, quiet, formal, prefers solitary activities, slow to warm up	Somewhat reserved, hangs back, leisurely pace, content with routine	Flexible, works well with individuals and groups, average pace, likes occasional stimulation, moderately cheerful	Enjoys teams, warm (a toucher), assertive, energetic, craves stimulation	Prefers group situations, life of party, forceful, dominant, cheerful, optimistic, very energetic	
Sensitivity	Resists change, trouble being empathic, somewhat intolerant of others' views, narrow interests	Focused on present, prefers concrete to abstract, likes efficiency, discounts feelings, strong values	Appreciates innovation & efficiency, tries new ways with evidence, likes a blend of new and familiar, cautiously responsive to others' feelings	Prefers variety, broad intellectual curiosity, accepting of others' beliefs & lifestyles, comfortable with theory	Attracted to novelty, seeks new ideas, responsive to others' feelings, trouble with routines	
					Total Score:	

CARES Assessment™ Results and Interpretation

Using the following Total Scores listing, match your total score from your Assessment answers to the total score range of the different Caregiver Types. Then go to the description for your Caregiver Type and read the interpretation that's unique for you.

Total Scores	Caregiver Type
14 and below	The Angry Man and The Lone Wolf
15–30	The Techno-Virtual Caregiver and The Lone Wolf
31–40	The Manager and The Worker
41 and above	The Perfectionist and The Manager

CARES Assessment Interpretation

You should have a sense of how your answers compare to the different caregiver types. Here are some descriptions of their caregiving strengths and weaknesses.

Caregiver Types

The Angry Man
Strengths
♦ Likely quite successful professionally and able to use those skills in his role as caregiver.

Weaknesses
♦ Feels frustration quite often.
♦ May take frustrations out on his care recipient.
♦ May act in a passive–aggressive manner to his care recipient.
♦ Not open to new information because of the anger and resentment regarding his own losses.

The Lone Wolf
Strengths
♦ Devoted to his role as a caregiver.
♦ Perseverance; will hang on in the role much longer than most.
♦ Genuinely wants to do his best in the role of caregiver.
♦ Acts with certainty.

Weaknesses
♦ Not often very outgoing or social.
♦ Does not understand how to make good use of his social network.
♦ Is likely to be perceived as gruff (i.e., "my way or the highway").
♦ Not open to advice from others—feels very certain about his own opinions.

The Techno-Virtual Caregiver
Strengths
- Enjoys innovation.
- Seeks support system to help make caregiving survivable.

Weaknesses
- May lack the necessary social graces needed to obtain help.
- Non-traditional to the point of ignoring tried-and-true resources.

The Manager
Strengths
- Confident in his skill to direct others.
- Excellent social skills.
- Pragmatic.
- Delegates tasks.

Weaknesses
- Puts severe limits on what he is willing to do as a caregiver.
- Likely perceived by friends or family as cold and unemotional.

The Worker

Strengths

- ♦ Enjoys camaraderie and seeks a support system.
- ♦ Open to advice.
- ♦ Cooperative.
- ♦ Can function well as a caregiver when provided the right kinds of information.

Weaknesses

- ♦ Does not ask a lot of questions.
- ♦ May defer to authority; this is a problem when caregiving feeds into isolation.
- ♦ Often unassertive; this may prevent him from finding answers.

The Perfectionist

Strengths

- ♦ Hard worker.
- ♦ Excellent with hands-on care because he wants it done right.

Weaknesses

- ♦ Finds fault easily; unforgiving of self and others.
- ♦ Has difficulty trusting.
- ♦ May complain too much because he feels out of control in caregiving.

Note to reader: Your defined CARES Assessment results do not have to match your actual behavior. The results merely describe your natural preferences. We all have the ability to choose behaviors that will enhance personal satisfaction and create better balance. Your CARES Assessment is not a prison; it is a foundation on which to build improved relationships and better quality of life. Regardless of how alone a caregiver feels, it is essential that he allows people into his network to provide care. This network includes anyone from doctors to neighbors.

We understand everyone is different and will probably have some aspect of each of the Caregiver Types described above. However, this Assessment is only intended to give you a starting point for thinking about your own caregiving style, strengths and weaknesses. We will be interested in hearing about your responses and thoughts on our website: **www.MaleGuideForCaregiving.com**

———

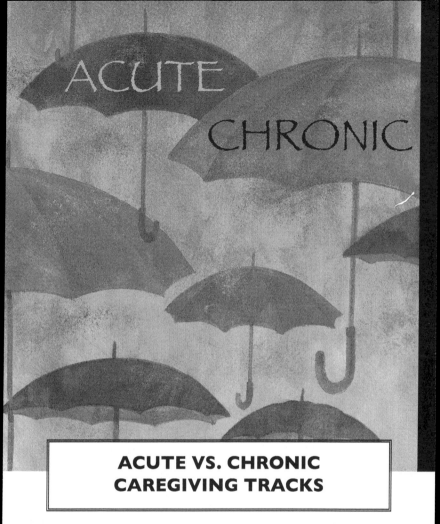

ACUTE VS. CHRONIC CAREGIVING TRACKS

Now that you have identified one or two caregiving styles and some of your personal strengths and weaknesses as a caregiver, it is time to define and explore your specific kind of caregiving situation.

What is Acute Care?

Acute care usually lasts one year or less. In an acute caregiving situation, either complete recovery or the end of life can be a matter of weeks or months. For example, to qualify for hospice care, a patient needs to have a six-month terminal diagnosis. Acute care means providing intensive care, but for a limited length of time.

Many serious conditions may be considered acute and require an informal caregiver:

♦ Heart attacks
♦ Broken bones
♦ Wounds
♦ Strokes
♦ Terminal diseases such as cancer

What is Chronic Care?

By definition, a chronic disease or condition persists for a long time, usually lasting one year or more. Chronic diseases generally cannot be prevented by vaccines or cured by medication, nor do they just disappear. Most chronic conditions end by becoming acute. Eighty-eight percent of Americans over 65 years of age have at least one chronic health condition. These include:

♦ Dementia/Alzheimer's
♦ Parkinson's
♦ Huntington's
♦ HIV/AIDS
♦ Chronic fatigue
♦ Rheumatoid arthritis and osteoarthritis
♦ Chronic respiratory diseases such as chronic obstructive pulmonary disease, and asthma pulmonary hypertension
♦ Chronic renal failure

- ◆ Diabetes mellitus
- ◆ Chronic hepatitis
- ◆ Autoimmune diseases
- ◆ Epilepsy
- ◆ Osteoporosis
- ◆ Sickle cell anemia

Because it is not always immediately obvious whether your caregiving situation is acute (short-term) or chronic (long-term), the first thing you need to do is ask a medical professional to tell you whether they feel you are going to be involved with an acute or chronic condition. Here are key questions you should ask:

- ◆ Is this a time-limited care situation?
- ◆ How likely is full recovery?
- ◆ At what rate will the recovery process proceed?
- ◆ How long will the patient be dependent on the physical presence of a caregiver, and then how long will the patient require occasional assistance?
- ◆ How long will it be until the patient is likely to recover fully?
- ◆ Is this a chronic care situation where there is no cure on the horizon?
- ◆ How long will the patient likely survive? That is, will this illness or injury result in premature death or will the patient require care throughout a normal life span?
- ◆ Is it likely that the care requirements will ever change, and if so, how and when?

We know that most men do not like ambiguity. We also know that many medical professionals are reluctant to

provide specific information, particularly when it comes
to a terminal diagnosis. You want to know exactly what
you are dealing with, and what to expect. The
professionals know some men are inclined to leap
immediately into problem-solving before they fully
understand the problem, so they are cautious about what
they say to patients and their male caregivers.

You need to do everything you can to persuade the doctor
or nurse to define acute vs. chronic care and, to the extent
they are willing, to find out what will be involved in each
track. This is an important first step in determining how
you will approach caregiving.

There are also significant differences in the strategies men
need to use in managing an acute or a chronic caregiving
situation. These include:

♦ The type of care a man is personally willing to provide
♦ The ratio of care provided by the man vs. care
  delegated to someone else
♦ The degree of personal sacrifice the man is willing to
  make
♦ The amount of out-of-pocket money the man is
  willing to spend on equipment/supplies
♦ The likelihood that the man will ask relatives and
  close friends for help
♦ The amount of research and seeking of second
  opinions launched by the caregiver
♦ The likelihood that the male caregiver will seek solace
  in outside relationships

The following checklist should help you make the decision about whether you are on an acute or chronic caregiving track. Did you get:

❑ An accurate, written diagnosis of the problem experienced by the care recipient?

❑ A comprehensive understanding of the anticipated course of the illness, including prognosis, or reality of recovery? This should include benchmarks along the way (if there are any), medical treatments or medications required, and statistics regarding how patients in similar situations fare. Some medical professionals recommend social workers to help caregivers access and identify resources.

❑ Information about insurance or governmental resources available to help defray the expenses of treatment or to cover medical supplies and equipment?

❑ Information about respite support available, and information on support groups for those caring for patients who share the illness or injury of your care recipient?

❑ An understanding with the care recipient to ensure they understand what is in store for them and to determine their expectations regarding their care provider? It is important for them to know that one of the options that must be considered is going to an assisted-living facility that takes patients for short term care and respite stays.

If you were able to check the five spaces above, you are ready to walk down either the acute or chronic caregiving track. (We do recommend you read both tracks because there are many crossover situations resulting from acute and chronic conditions.)

The Acute Track

When a man realizes he is in an acute care situation, he knows, one way or the other, that there is going to be a light at the end of the tunnel.

The implications are:

♦ He can continue to make long-range plans
♦ He can afford to put large amounts of energy into caregiving because there is a time limit and he knows that he can ultimately recharge his batteries
♦ He will want to put a lot of energy into the relationship, which will bear fruit when the caregiving phase of the illness/injury is over (especially if the patient is his wife)
♦ He will be willing to provide a large percentage of the care personally in order to save money and to keep the relationship as fresh and viable as possible

Acute Caregiving Suggestions Based On Your Caregiver Type

The Lone Wolf caregiver is not gregarious and does not normally seek advice or support from others. He will be inclined to do everything himself and runs significant risk of burnout. His best course of action is to find someone immediately to help with caregiving duties and to leave the area when the alternate caregiver is on duty.

The Angry Man caregiver will have to be especially careful to build extra interpersonal support for himself; he will need plenty of reassurance that he is not failing to provide adequate care. He might consider a male support group or lunching with friends at work so he can blow off steam and get some reassurance from people who care about him.

The Manager caregiver should, in consultation with the care recipient, divide up the caregiving duties between what he will provide and what he will delegate to others. If he does too much personally, he may feel he has been demoted and begin to resent low-level caregiving tasks.

The Worker caregiver should seek out information about the illness or injury beyond what he has been given, and the Internet makes this possible. There is security in learning as much as possible about the illness/injury of his care recipient. He needs to be advised on a regular basis, and should immediately identify someone to play that role, even if a fee is involved. The role could be filled by a counselor or a certified care manager.

The Perfectionist caregiver will have trouble living up to his own high standards. One way to deal with this dilemma is for the perfectionist to draft a comprehensive caregiving manual and training program that defines his preferences. Then he could arrange for respite caregivers to go through an initiation process with the caregiver as trainer and coach before the respite period begins. This would help the caregiver maintain control and give him the confidence that his standards are being maintained during respite periods.

The Techno-Virtual caregiver is typically a younger, media-savvy man and will find an appropriate venue for a high-tech and "high-touch" style with the acute caregiving situation. Since he is not afraid to devote personal time to his caregiving chores, he can jump right into short-term caregiving tasks while on the lookout for technological tools that will make his job easier or provide more comfort for his care recipient. Because the Techno-Virtual caregiver thrives on seeing actual beginnings and endings and appreciates measurable outcomes over a specific length of time, he is likely to be an effective acute caregiver.

The Chronic Track

When a man realizes that the caregiving role is chronic (i.e., long-term or even permanent), it is essential that he ration the amount of energy he puts into the role. Because it is difficult to see light at the end of the tunnel, he must learn to pace himself to minimize the potential for burnout. He needs straightforwardly to address some of the important issues the chronic track raises:

♦ He cannot afford to respond immediately to every request. This pattern would be less troublesome in acute care, but in chronic care the potential for burnout is huge.

♦ He needs to be careful about making long-range plans because he simply does not know what his responsibilities will be. As a caregiver to a wife, her limitations will indefinitely impact his flexibility to travel, socialize, and play. The caregiver will need to discuss this potential isolation with his wife, and make plans to minimize adverse consequences.

♦ Relationship management will take a different path in chronic caregiving because the effort to keep his life somewhat normal will have more significance here than in the acute track.

♦ He must recognize that he is now a candidate for caregiver burnout and plan to ration the energy he devotes to caring for his care recipient, balancing the recipient's needs against his own needs.

♦ He must put his own *needs* above the *wants and desires* of his care recipient. His endurance as a care provider depends on it.

♦ He must immediately locate resources to share the burden of care. He should consider home health care, private-duty nurses, day care programs, or hiring neighbors as sitters.

♦ He must put aside any prejudices he has against nursing homes and assisted living facilities and begin to consider such placement as a viable alternative, even if only for respite stays.

Chronic Caregiving Suggestions Based on Your Caregiver Type

The Lone Wolf caregiver is at an immediate disadvantage delivering chronic care. He is not accustomed to sharing the workload. His bias for doing it all himself is dangerous to his health, and he will have to work especially hard to overcome his reluctance to accept help. Perhaps it would help if he approached one of the few people he has come to trust professionally and seek their ideas about what options he should consider. Someone should warn him against trying to go it alone. It could be deadly.

The Angry Man caregiver is also reluctant to obtain help from others. He might be inclined to take out some of his frustrations on the care recipient. He likely has experienced past career success, but the problem-solving he used successfully at work does not seem to be helping in this situation. This man desperately needs some interpersonal support, whether from family and friends or from a support group. As is the case with the Lone Wolf, working in isolation is fraught with danger for the Angry Man. He needs to swallow his pride and ask for help.

The Manager caregiver has an immediate advantage going into a chronic care scenario. It will feel natural to him to orchestrate a team approach to providing care, using whatever resources are within reach. The Manager also knows to communicate expectations clearly to the team and to evaluate team members' care (you have to inspect what you expect).

The Worker caregiver will be inclined to drive himself crazy seeking ever more information about the chronic condition of the patient, hoping to find evidence that will overturn the existing prognosis. Eventually the Worker will need to stop this investigation, accept the diagnostic parameters, and get on with finding some acceptable balance in his life for the long haul.

The Techno-Virtual caregiver will find chronic caregiving more difficult, in part because of his youth. The ambiguities of chronic conditions, the lack of clear results coming from treatments or medications, and the inability of technology or even the best information available to substantially change his situation will frustrate him. He will need to look at technology in a different way. He might access relaxation exercises on the web or use his social networks to share frustrating moments and ask for advice. He may need to consult with older chronic caregivers or just another older person to get a sense of how they have dealt with frustrating situations. Finally, the Techno-Virtual caregiver might begin recording his own experiences in chronic care so that others in a similar situation can learn from his experiences.

———

CAREGIVER MYTHS AND REALITIES

A myth is a popular belief that has become associated with a person or an institution. It is a fiction or a half-truth. Over the years of dealing with caretaking and caregivers, we have found a number of myths which, if subscribed to, can make caregiving harder and can lead to growing frustrations and fatigue.

Our human desire to fit in also helps perpetuate caregiving mythology and pressures caregivers to live in potentially unhealthy situations. For many individual situations, there is no real place to find real help and untangle the myths or clichés that many caregivers live by.

Myth: Men will ask the hard caregiving questions.
Male caregivers in the midst of a crisis often defer to doctors and other health care professionals. They often do not ask enough critical questions about either their care recipient or themselves.

Older generations of male caregivers have been taught to respect physicians, but the truth is that medical doctors are technicians, and many of them have limited experience looking at the big picture of a complex caregiving scenario. They also make mistakes.

Younger generations like Boomers and the Diversity Generation are often more skeptical of medical authority because they have unfettered access to medical information via the Internet. Men who are somewhat intimidated by physicians will have a harder time asking the tough questions and demanding answers.

No matter how unnatural it might feel, men need to demand complete honesty from their doctors or other health care professionals about what they can and cannot expect in their particular caregiving situation. Then the male caregiver needs to seek answers from other resources if his main medical source of information clearly does not have acceptable answers. We strongly support the concept of personal health and caregiving literacy and the value of seeking second opinions. Doing so makes us much better caregivers.

Myth: The public is disdainful of ill or handicapped people.

Obviously we cannot speak for all male caregivers, but they often express concern about what their friends, co-workers, family, and the even the general public will think about them, or their loved one, when they are out in public.

Acting on anxiety about how others perceive you can lead to social isolation. It is not just that going out of the house takes a great deal of planning (which it does), but concern about what others think is an unnecessary additional burden to carry.

The man whose mother or wife has Alzheimer's may not leave the house with her because she might "misbehave, and then what will people think about me?" The bottom line is that social conformity is a caregiver's enemy.

More Myths and Realities

What support resources—your family and friends—tell you may inadvertently hurt you. The italicized statements below are some typical "gems" of informal advice. The statements in parenthesis are typical caregiver internal reactions.

"Hang in there." (That's all I can do!)

"Things could be worse; look on the bright side." (Worse? I guess I could have leprosy.)

"You are lucky to spend so much time with your loved one." (Really? Would you want to trade?)

"I don't know if I could do what you do." (I am no hero!)

"You have so much strength!" (No, really I do not—I am weak, I cry, I scream, and I sometimes hate my life! Do not make me feel more guilt for wanting out of this!)

This "advice" can encourage male caregivers to "suck it up" and stay the course because of what society expects of them. They get the message that to ask for help or seek an alternative course means they are weak for wanting a life of their own.

Here are a few more myths, paired with observations from the real world of caregiving:

Myth	Reality
Commitments to care for a loved one are forever	When we commit to deliver care, there is no way we could have known how bad it could get—we did not read the fine print, because there was none. If we had known, we might not have made the same commitment to provide care. Many people get trapped into this commitment by a dying parent or spouse, leveraging the caregiver to take up the load. In those moments, we are pressured to agree to something we might not have fully and clearly considered.
The needs of the ill person are more important than the needs of the caregiver	If the needs of the caregiver are not satisfied, then there might be nothing left for the care recipient.
There is something noble about sacrificing your life for a loved one	Martyrdom only works after death. Is this the caregiver's intention? Probably it is not.
The ill person's needs and wants are equally important	No, they are not. The caregiver's needs are much more important than the wants of the care recipient.
It is wrong to be selfish	Being selfish is sometimes a requirement to survive caregiving. Caregivers must take time for themselves. "No" is not a bad word.
Blood is thicker than water	The relationships we create and nurture are ever so much more valuable to us than the ones we inherit. Unless you are able to mute or tone down the mandatory or obligatory qualities of a relationship with a relative and replace them with genuine mutual compassion, this relationship is less valuable than a close friendship.
	If we end up caring for a parent or relative who has a history of ignoring our needs, or even abusing us, do we not have the right to ask if we really owe them our own lives as their caregiver?

Myth	Reality
Wedding vows mean exactly what they say— "in sickness and in health, for richer or for poorer," and "till death do us part."	For spousal caregivers in particular, many never understood how sick or how poor it is possible to be. If we had known, would we have taken the vow? It makes sense to negotiate and develop a "new normal" relationship contract with your spouse or anyone else you are caring for. If the person is not mentally competent, then the well partner has all the power and must act in a manner that is best and realistic for both of them.
We must show unconditional love toward our loved ones	All human love comes with conditions. There are no exceptions.
Always tell the truth	While we do not promote lying, we understand that massaging or putting a spin on the truth is sometimes the only way caregivers can carve out time to meet their own needs.
In a conflict, someone always gets hurt	Conflict can be positive and, when mixed with honesty and love, it sometimes creates unexpectedly positive resolutions.

Men who are making sacrifices to care for a loved one often criticize themselves for wanting to have their own needs and wants met. Society has taught (brainwashed?) us to believe that it is somehow wrong to be selfish sometimes. The actual origin of this social programming begins at birth. Infants can only think of themselves, and as children mature, parents attempt to counteract this form of self-centeredness by promoting the opposite idea—that the needs of others are more important than their own.

Those on the periphery of caregiving often promote the idea that the caregiver should feel guilty for rebelling against these sacrifices. We often suspect that these observers have a hidden agenda, such as "do not ask me to help you." Men must listen to their own gut rather than listening to those who do not have a dog in this fight.

The truth is that caregivers who do not pay attention to their own needs can become useless to their loved ones. Men must stop believing the "it is wrong to be selfish" mythology or they themselves will need a caregiver.

———

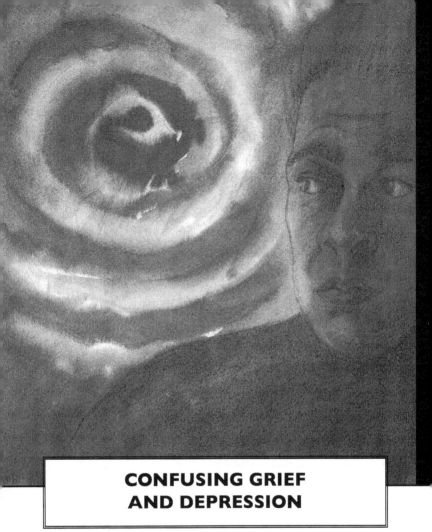

CONFUSING GRIEF
AND DEPRESSION

Men are reputed to be more logical than women, and more in control of their emotions. There is not much truth in this stereotype. The truth is, we have found that many caregiving men start out by rationalizing their feelings and repressing their anger, guilt, and feelings of inadequacy. This rationalization can lead to a dangerous and confused emotional state.

For example, many men who are caregivers confuse depression and grief. It is important for a male caregiver to understand the difference. Depression is usually characterized by complete and utter feelings of hopelessness. Extreme depression can originate from a chemical imbalance resulting from a traumatic situation or hereditary factors; this kind of depression can be treated with medication.

However, if these kinds of feelings last for more than two weeks, depression can lead to a variety of emotional and physical problems. Many men report having trouble performing normal day-to-day activities, and feel as if life is not worth living.

Grief is also a multi-faceted response to loss, particularly to the loss of someone close. Some men report they find themselves experiencing a loss of their old lifestyle with the person they are now caring for. This kind of grief can also involve intense emotional suffering.

Whatever a male caregiver calls his mood, sadness and grieving is normal. Caregiving brings about a broad array of emotions, which frequently includes short periods of grief and depression. He is not just sad, or grieving for his loved one's losses, but for his own loss. It is helpful for men to try to identify patterns in their emotional response to caregiving.

Grief can lead to depression and depression can include grieving. It is not normal to feel depressed or to grieve for an indefinite amount of time. When these feelings persist, professional help can bring the caregiver some emotional relief.

We should be focused on preventing severe and continuing depression while caregiving. Sadly, male caregivers are more likely to feel despondent than their female counterparts. Some have even killed their loved ones and then themselves, apparently believing that there was no relief in sight.

This is a plea for men to seek alternatives before acting in destructive ways. There are places to go for help:

- ◆ The organization that is associated with your loved one's illness (i.e., Alzheimer's Association, MS Society, etc.)
- ◆ County mental health services
- ◆ Your physician
- ◆ NAMI – National Alliance on Mental Illness

On a more positive note, men do not attempt suicide as often as women. However, when they do attempt suicide, they are four times more likely to succeed in killing themselves. These poignant statistics are extremely important to all male caregivers because knowing and recognizing the signs and symptoms of depression and dangerous emotions is essential to knowing when you are nearing your "tipping point" or nearing the point of losing your balance, and need to take actions for your own well-being.

Signs of Depression

Signs and symptoms of depression can vary, but the following is a general guide. You might start by asking the simple question: What is my mood right now? Here are some early signs of depression from the Mayo Clinic:

♦ Feelings of sadness or unhappiness
♦ Irritability or frustration, even over small matters
♦ Loss of interest or pleasure in normal activities
♦ Reduced sex drive
♦ Insomnia or excessive sleeping
♦ Changes in appetite—depression often causes decreased appetite and weight loss, but in some people it causes increased cravings for food and weight gain
♦ Agitation or restlessness; for example, pacing, hand-wringing, or an inability to sit still
♦ Slowed thinking, speaking, or body movements
♦ Indecisiveness, distractibility, and decreased concentration
♦ Fatigue, tiredness, and loss of energy—even small tasks may seem to require a lot of effort
♦ Feelings of worthlessness or guilt, fixating on past failures, or blaming yourself when things aren't going right
♦ Trouble thinking, concentrating, making decisions, and remembering things
♦ Frequent thoughts of death, dying, or suicide
♦ Crying spells for no apparent reason
♦ Unexplained physical problems such as back pain or headaches

The reality here is that men do need to get in touch with their emotions as caregivers. Emotions will always trump logic. Most importantly, you can never become a balanced and healthy caregiver if you are unbalanced emotionally.

There might be myths that you encounter on a daily basis that we have not covered here. If there are, you need to identify and counteract these myths in a way that sustains you. Remember, if you are not well, you will not be able to care for someone else.

———

CONSIDER YOUR GENERATIONAL GROUP

Another way to learn more about your caregiving style is to consider your own generational values and actions. Most of the men reading this Guide will come from one of four generations. You can see what generation you come from by asking yourself: Was I born before 1932 (the GI or Civic Generation), between 1932–1944 (the Mediating or Adaptive Generation), 1945–1963 (Boomers), or finally, 1964–1981(Diversity or GenX Generation)?

Here is a very short review of each generation and the caregiving styles we have associated with that generation:

Note: *Please read all of the descriptions. We are all influenced not only by our generation but by the generations with whom we interact every day.*

The GI or Civic Generation Caregiver
(born 1931 or earlier)

(GI stands for "General Infantry" from World War II).
This generation came out of a predominantly agricultural economy and many of them lived as adolescents and young adults through the Great Depression. Many of them were heroes in a great hour of national crisis, World War II.

After the war these young men helped create many of the national and international corporations and institutions we know today. These are no-nonsense, quiet, frugal men. They get the most out of their resources and they respect a clear chain of command, based mostly on their military experience.

This man is not afraid to do the "dirty work" of caregiving because he has seen so much worse in his past.

Above all else, the GI caregiver is extremely loyal to those he loves and cares for. He knows what it took to live in hard times and to fight under horrible battle conditions. He also truly believes in "till death do us part."

When we see male caregivers from this generation, we often see two dominant types:

The Lone Wolf

This man is likely devoted to his role as a caregiver. He will continue in the caregiving role much longer than most (sometimes too long). He genuinely wants to do his best in the role of caregiver. This man is often not very outgoing. He does not always understand how to make good use of his social network. Caregiving responsibilities have isolated and separated this generational caregiver from most of what society views as a "healthy and active life," so he may feel frustrated as an older man and as a caregiver.

Others are likely to perceive him as gruff ("my way or the highway"), and not open to advice. He tends not to question his own beliefs. The Lone Wolf is often left on the caregiving battlefield without much support.

The Worker

This man is often looking for someone to agree with how he is caring for his loved one. But he doesn't ask a lot of questions because he naturally defers to authority—in World War II there were far more privates, corporals, and sergeants than officers. Soldiers, sailors, airmen, and marines respected the chain of command.

This man is often unassertive and this prevents him from finding answers; that is why he seems always to be searching. On the positive side, this GI caregiver is open to advice and with the right support system, he is cooperative and can function well as a caregiver—if he is provided with good information.

The Adaptive Generation Caregiver
(born between 1932–1944)

The majority of men from this generation came of age too late for World War II and were also born too early to feel the pressures and burdens of the Vietnam War. These men were the unobtrusive children of depression and war, and the conformist "Lonely Crowd" generation. They worked quietly behind the GI heroes and developed much of the social infrastructure we have in our country today. They supply the highest percentage of volunteers in America of any living generation.

While somewhat hierarchical in their outlook, these men differed with their GI counterparts by seeing work issues as more complex. They developed the concept of seeking excellence in the workplace, and sensed the need for a more nuanced approach to management as a younger and more racially diverse generation of workers began to enter the workforce. This generation was primarily responsible for formalizing human resources as a legitimate organizational function.

These men will also quietly do the dirty work of caregiving but feel emotionally frustrated that they cannot find or afford someone else to do it. Like their GI counterparts, they are also very loyal.

Below are two types of male caregivers we often find in this generation.

The Manager

He is confident that he can direct others, and he has a highly developed set of social skills. While extremely loyal, he is also more pragmatic and can put clear limits on what he is willing to do as a caregiver. Consequently, he could be perceived by friends and family as cold and unemotional.

He might find a "Plan B" (finding someone else to provide care) easier after reaching his tipping point and see it as just another form of delegation.

He is also likely to cultivate a comforting relationship outside the home (i.e., he will not allow caregiving to destroy his social outlets).

The Angry Man

This type is the flip side of the Adaptive Generation caregiver. He feels very frustrated because even though he has been an active volunteer and made many contributions over the course of his life, he feels like nobody is there or wants to help him right now. Potentially, he feels "owed." If this continues, he can become unappreciative and increasingly less sociable.

Often he is not open to new knowledge. This can leave him angry about his caregiving situation because he will most certainly make mistakes.

Professionally this person is often a retired manager or a skilled technician (e.g., a mechanic, engineer, or programmer) and likely very successful. This leads to even more frustration at home if he believes he has shortcomings as a caregiver. He will often blame others or the care recipient for holding him back, or not giving him enough support.

The Boomer Male Caregiver
(born between 1945–1963)

The Baby Boomers are the largest generation (84 million if you count immigrants) in American history. They entered college and the workplace in large numbers from the Kennedy through the Reagan administrations. This group, raised in a culture of abundance, became the country's first large consumer generation. It has been heavily influenced by the media, especially television.

These were the babies of optimism and hubris. This was the generation of *change* because everything changed for them. When there is a need, Boomers believe there is probably a product or service to meet it (or that there should be).

Watching civil rights battles and the war in Vietnam on TV, this generation began at an early age to distrust authority and question the myths of their parents. In the workplace, they demanded creativity and meaning in their work, participation in decision-making, equality, and better training, and they saw the need for more risk-taking in approaches to solving problems.

The men of this generation also encountered strong, feminist women, and they are half of the largest divorced group in American history. This has resulted in complex mixed families with conflicting loyalties.

Today many men of this generation are part of what we call the "Sandwich Generation," taking care of their children, grandchildren, and parents simultaneously.

Here are the principal types of male caregivers we often find in this generation:

The Perfectionist
This man is most likely a workaholic. He often nitpicks and over-reacts to minor situations. He is a little more sensitive than his older male counterparts, but can find fault easily and does not trust much of the advice he receives. He is suspicious of authority. Therefore, he might not be getting the kind of help he really needs.

The people who have tried to help him have turned away because of his complaining. He knows there are many options out there—he has done much of his research on the Internet—and believes he has access to the "right" answers. He wonders why medical and caregiving professionals, and the care recipient, do not simply follow his direction. He can be very unforgiving.

On the positive side, this male caregiver does not usually make hands-on care mistakes and has likely mastered the economics of his health-care situation. He does not like to be doing all of the dirty work of caregiving but will do it if he cannot find or afford other help.

The Manager (with a Boomer Twist)

This man is confident that he can direct others in giving care. He has often worked on teams and understands how powerful groups can be if they work together. However, despite highly developed social skills, he can get lost in the process of getting things done.

Because he is not as loyal in the traditional sense as his male elders, he can put strict limits on what he is willing to do as a caregiver. Consequently, he is often perceived as cold and unemotional.

He might find a Plan B (alternative care arrangements) easier after reaching his tipping point, but he may define it as a logical outcome of his ability to successfully manage his caregiving tasks. He might even find this change easier because his working life has involved continuous change. Intellectually and emotionally, he will be able to see relinquishing some of his major caregiving duties as part of a natural transition process.

It is likely that he will find a relationship outside of caregiving in which to take comfort rather than allowing caregiving to limit his social contacts.

The Diversity or Gen X Caretaker
(born between 1964–1981)

These were the first babies to come of age in a society with rapidly increasing divorce rates, experimental education practices, latchkey programs, an AIDS-influenced dating scene, birth control, kids with weapons, and increasing numbers of young people committing suicide. This generation has the most experience with a multicultural, multi-racial society. Proficiency with technology comes as naturally to this generation as the air they breathe.

They get along very well with the GI generation but not so well with their Mediating and Boomer parents. The reason grandchildren get along so well with grandparents is that they both have a common enemy! Skipping a generation sometimes helps in better communication.

Members of this generation see themselves as self-sufficient, self-starting, and naturally entrepreneurial. They show little loyalty to the companies they work for (having seen many of their parents lose 20- and 30-year jobs through restructuring), are skeptical about group process, slogans, and name brands, and eschew political correctness. They put a much higher value on their personal time and private lives than their three older counterparts.

Here is the principal type of emerging male caregiver we find in this generation:

The Techno-Virtual Caregiver

This caregiver is looking to be high-tech and high-touch. He is on Facebook or some other virtual community asking for advice from his caregiver counterparts. He probably avoids more traditional caregiving websites, resources, and support groups because there are usually few people like him in those groups or organizations.

He is not afraid to devote personal time to his caregiving chores because he always puts family and personal matters ahead of work, but he is always on the lookout for technological caregiving help to support his personal commitment.

This male caregiver will be more open to multicultural caregiving help because he is the first generation in U.S. history to experience incredible diversity in schools, playgrounds, and community centers. He lives in a shrinking and interdependent world.

He can appear stand-offish and aloof because he spends so much time with electronic media, but with people he loves, he is warm and generous. If you can show him a better path for caregiving, he is frequently open to try something new.

Importance of Generational Awareness

Why is your generation important? Consider this cross-generational, real caregiving story:

Born in 1940, Nancy needs to take an antidepressant, but she continually refuses, stating that she is not "crazy." Her son (born in 1970) is exhausted by her continual refusal to take her medicine. Nancy refuses to believe that the antidepressant was prescribed to control her pain, not her depression. Her parents were not comfortable with psychology as a legitimate profession, nor did they believe in therapeutic interventions associated with mental health issues. They were a couple who believed in "picking yourself up by your bootstraps" and believed "happy pills" were for weak people. Accordingly, Nancy was non-compliant based on her own generational core values.

As her son began to understand why his mother was so angry and non-compliant, he asked the prescribing doctor to educate his mother on the use of the antidepressant as a form of pain relief. Through this educational process his mother's fears began to subside.

It is important to understand why our parents or grandparents act the way they do.

Do they have a long-standing bias against taking medications?

Some older individuals are not comfortable with the

advances in medicine and may mistakenly fear side effects (such as addiction). The solution is to educate the care recipient about responsible use of the drugs.

Are they worried about the expense and therefore attempting to ration the medications?
The care recipient may not understand how the insurance works and may also have concerns about finances. The solution is to explain how the medications are being paid for.

Do they need more education from the health care professionals as to why they need the medication?
Some patients simply did not fully understand their doctor's explanation and need more information. The solution is to take time to teach the care recipient about his or her diagnosis and the role of prescribed medications. This information is probably more credible when delivered by the doctor.

Removing these barriers will make the quality of life better for both the caregiver and the care recipient.

Some care recipients are more compliant if their medication is administered by someone other than the caregiver—a home health aide, neighbor, or friend. The social graces will often take over and improve cooperation.

———

WHAT IS YOUR TIPPING POINT?

Everyone has at least one "tipping point" in his or her life. It is a time when events—normally negative ones—accumulate or mount up to a degree that a situation becomes intolerable. These tipping points normally lead to some kind of significant life change. Sometimes a person may miss the tipping point itself; a late or delayed realization can be quite a shock.

This Guide strives to help you recognize what might be happening to you in your caretaking before you actually reach your tipping point. Once you arrive, we can recommend how you can make clear and informed decisions for yourself and your loved one.

A Tipping Point Case Study

Earl was in his early sixties and started out his caregiving duties feeling like he had everything under control. After all, he reasoned, he had run his own business for years and was an experienced manager. Since this man also had financial resources, he could always hire extra help when he needed to.

He was very well organized. He used his computer to remind him about his wife's medication schedule and his schedule of caregiving duties. He even took days off from caregiving because he was told that good caregivers needed rest. What our friend was not aware of was the establishment of a pattern of little frustrations, which he ignored, that eventually led to his tipping point.

His wife Emily had had an early onset of vascular dementia, one of the most common forms of dementia, ranking only second to Alzheimer's disease. Vascular dementia is caused by chronic, reduced blood flow to the brain, usually as the result of a stroke or series of strokes. In many cases, the strokes are so small that the sufferer may not notice any symptoms. But over time the damage adds up, leading to memory loss, confusion, and other signs of dementia. By the time Earl and Emily obtained an accurate diagnosis, Emily was quite limited in what she could do on her own. Soon, she couldn't eat, dress, or even use the bathroom by herself. To this couple, it seemed to happen suddenly. A seemingly healthy woman in her early sixties suddenly became a person with tremors, loss of bowel control, and significant memory loss. She experienced terrible confusion at night, and seemed to get worse every day. There is no known cure for vascular dementia and the time span of its progression varies significantly.

Earl promised that he would make sure she stayed in their home and that he would care for her himself. He was not sure if she really understood his promise, but she did smile and calm down a bit when he told her. He closed his office but was able to work from home. He arranged for supplemental help and began doing everything he could to make sure his wife was protected and comfortable.

After several months he began noticing changes in himself. Because they were minor, he did not pay much attention; he wrote these changes off to what comes along with the caretaking territory. He figured he just needed to "man up" to the challenge and things would work out.

He found he was losing patience with old clients, and his business started slowing down. This created financial pressures that he had not experienced in years. In spite of his best efforts at taking care of himself, he found himself beginning to take over-the-counter sleeping pills to avoid hearing his wife's moaning during the night. Some of his golfing friends observed the deepening dark circles under his eyes. He would often sit and stare at the TV and think about the plans he and his wife had had for travel and adventure. This made him feel depressed. But more significantly, he found himself treating Emily more and more like an object. The routine of cleaning her up after an "accident" made him feel less like a husband and more like a hired attendant.

So in spite of doing everything right by the currently accepted caregiver standards, our friend found himself one day losing it and standing by his wife's bed, crying and yelling at her uncontrollably. She just smiled at him as he sank to the floor. He now knew he had had enough and could not care for her at home any longer.

The Boiling Frog Syndrome

One defining concept of caregiving is the imperceptible increase in *sacrifice*. This makes it especially difficult to recognize that you are at your tipping point. Men as caregivers rarely anticipate many of the deep sacrifices they will be making. Caregiving quickly becomes a way of life and men often state later that they were clueless about the toll it took on them. They allowed their lives to become devoid of all pleasure and wondered how it all happened.

How does it happen? Sometimes the process is called the "boiling frog" syndrome. As cold-blooded creatures, frogs adapt to temperature changes automatically. As this metaphor goes, one can place a frog in a pot of cold water, put the pot on the stove, and without alarming the frog, increase the heat. The temperature gradually rises to the point that the frog dies—but because of its adaptive nature, it never realized its danger.

Male caregivers are often not aware that they are not satisfying their own needs. Eventually they reach the point at which the care recipient benefits but only at the expense of the caregiver.

Caregiving can be isolating. On bad days, "unacceptable" thoughts (anger, frustration, regret) creep in and there is no place to express them. Only other caregivers would recognize, accept, and understand desperate pleas and angry expressions of frustration. That is why support groups—formal or informal—are important.

Caregivers to sick spouses start to wonder how long they can live this way and how to stop feeling as if they are losing their minds. Healthy spousal caregivers wonder how long they can deliver constant care, wonder if they are ever going to have fun again, wonder if they can remain celibate and true to their vows. They feel internal pressures building. They want to scream that they have had enough of the doctor appointments, the hospital visits, wiping up, distributing medicines, dressing wounds—and that they cannot take it anymore. Then, of course, they wonder if all that means they are a bad person.

Often, those caring for a spouse never dreamed, when they got married, that they would someday look at the person who once was "the love of my life" and think, "Did I ever love her?" When he finds himself in this untenable situation, the well spouse reviews his wedding vows with a new sense of questioning. "How devoted was I, what did it all mean, and can I do it anymore?" "Would my spouse be doing the same for me if I were the one who was ill? Would I even expect her to?"

Many healthy husbands feel like they are in constant mourning, yet there has been no death. The wife is alive and in the same home. The loss is constantly present and the worst of it is that these men are so lonely they lose some of their capacity for empathy and stop resonating with their wife's losses. Some men report feeling guilty for grieving their own losses. The healthy man may even conclude that he is "just being selfish."

Some male caregivers with minor children in the home feel like single parents despite the physical presence of their wives. Other caregivers watch their lives disappear as their best friend or parent slowly becomes a dependent ward. For those caregivers who did not have a great relationship before the disability arrived, the diminished life feels like a prison sentence. But of course, to most men it is not "acceptable" to voice these feelings.

Male caregivers grieve that their lives, as they knew them, are gone. They grieve that illness and disability came in and stole their hopes and dreams. It is heart-wrenching to wake up one day and realize that the dreams you shared with your spouse are now unattainable. Living without hopes and dreams feels like a form of death. Nothing about becoming a spousal caregiver is how they envisioned their future. They have lost control of their lives.

This is the point at which Plan B must be considered.

Plan B

Plan B is an alternative strategy when the preferred course of action has not worked. Many men will discuss their Plan B as if it is a last resort. They will use it when all else fails, when they are too exhausted to care for their loved one any longer.

The challenge for the reader in this section is to understand that many caregivers already have their own informal Plan B ready, but only in the event of their own demise. They have mentally answered the question, "What happens if I can no longer care for my loved one?" They may have begun to recognize that they are older and may not have the strength and stamina it takes to deliver care and supervision for an aging parent. Even if they have made a promise to care for their care recipient, they may instinctively know this cannot last forever because the price may be too high.

One barrier to Plan B preparation, mentioned above, is a promise made to the care recipient that "I will never put you in a nursing home." Normally such promises were made many years earlier, before there was any awareness of the present illness or disability. Promises like this represent real (if unintended) barriers to effective problem-solving.

In the first place, such promises are frequently made in the heat of emotion, such as when an aging parent is fearful for his or her future. The promise is intended as a kind of reassurance, but without much clear thinking about the implications of such a commitment.

Secondly, promises like these have a time stamp. At the time the promise is made, nursing home placement would seem far-fetched and unlikely to materialize. If there were an imminent need for alternative care, such a promise would be unlikely to be made. As situations change, commitments must be re-evaluated in light of present realities. "But you promised…" tugs at our heart strings, but there is a statute of limitations on ancient promises. All of our lives change when we become a caregiver and we need to be open to change even where there are old commitments.

We also need to remember that nursing homes and other intermediate care facilities are different today than they were when the "promise" was made. And the good news is that many are trying to improve nationwide.

Plan B often needs to be considered sooner rather than later, now instead of when a crisis develops. The reason for this suggestion is that for some, Plan B is a life-saver, a rescue from pain, and can restore warm loving feelings for the care recipient. Plan B should be initiated before exhaustion, anger, or death consumes the caregiver.

If Plan B consists of imagining a suitable retirement center, assisted living, or nursing home, explore those that are available in the local community. If Plan B consists of asking extended family members to rotate the caregiving responsibility, start talking to them *now* so that everyone is aware in advance of the possibility of change. Confronting the obstacles before the plan requires action is the best way to stay in control. This is a way of saving your sanity and preserving a future for youself.

The earlier example is applicable to a man caring for an aging parent. Frequently men demonstrate frustration at a parent in ways they could never have imagined. They get angry about the dirty counters when Mom tries to help in the kitchen, only to make a huge mess she cannot see. They yell because Dad has asked the same question for the hundredth time in a day. Then they feel guilty. Sometimes, even with the best of intentions, living together does not work out. Adult children have their own lives.

These are some examples of men who chose Plan B:

Jim

Jim said he felt no guilt for choosing a long-term care facility for his wife. After living like a zombie, going through the daily rituals of care, feeling short-tempered, and isolated all the time, he realized he needed to make a change because he was "losing precious time" with his wife Shirley. He did not want to be angry due to her poor memory and the demands that cleaning up after her required. He realized that he might precede her in death. Then who would care for her? This loving man realized that if he allowed professional caregivers to provide the hands-on, physical labor, he could then spend time with his wife "just loving her." He did not relinquish control as her caregiver because he still supervised her care. Instead, he was free to focus on the things that brought her joy and provided comfort. In making this decision to live apart, he was able to find peace while caring for his wife for as long as she was alive.

Steven

Sixty-three-year-old Steven expressed frustration over the difficulties of caring for his father. He said his wife had recently had open-heart surgery. While she has fully recovered, he fears his father will outlive his wife. He said they had made travel plans for when the kids were grown. Now he is angry that his caregiving will interfere with time he had hoped to spend with her. Steven said he did not know how to come to terms with "these selfish feelings." In discussing his Plan B, he began to feel better about choosing his wife and himself as his first priority, while knowing his father was living in an adult care home with people who were able to provide proper care and supervision. This son began to display the pride he really felt for his father's military honors and once again enjoyed their visits.

Plan B Questionnaire

These questions will help clarify the reader's thoughts about Plan B. This is a simulated professional interview, with multiple-choice options to help you articulate your thoughts about the issues.

1. On a bad caregiving day, my fantasy is that…
   _____.

   A. the care recipient lives in a long-term care facility.
   B. the care recipient gets well.
   C. the care recipient lives with another family member.
   D. the care recipient dies.
   E. Other.

2. When I think about my loved one's care options were I unable to deliver care, my thought is that…
   _____.

   A. my loved one would be admitted to a long-term facility.
   B. another family member would take over the responsibilities.
   C. I never considered this because I assume that I will outlive and remain healthier than the care recipient.
   D. I never considered the "what if" scenario because I do not have time.
   E. Other.

3. What portion(s) of Plan B are already in place?

  _____

  A. Funeral service/preparations are complete for the care recipient.
  B. Family members have assisted or offered respite.
  C. There is no one else to help, no plans made.
  D. I refuse to discuss other options.
  E. Other.

4. What obstacle(s) are keeping me from pursuing Plan B? _____

  A. Care recipient will be angry.
  B. I promised I would deliver care.
  C. It is my job, now.
  D. Care recipient needs only me.
  E. Other.

5. How would my relationship with the care recipient and my daily life improve if I chose Plan B now?

  _____

  A. It would get worse.
  B. It would improve.
  C. I could spend quality time with the care recipient.
  D. I would feel guilty.
  E. Other.

Now that you know about Plan B and that all of us have a tipping point, here is a quick assessment to see where you fall on the tipping point continuum. Answer these questions honestly...

Tipping Point Assessment

DIRECTIONS: Read the statements in the chart on the next page and answer them with a YES or NO. Add the total of your YES answers. Your total could be as low as 0, or as high as 15.

TIPPING POINT ASSESSMENT™	YES	NO
1. Do you have trouble going to sleep at night?		
2. Are you eating too much, or too little?		
3. Do you fantasize about becoming sick, or injured, so you would be cared for?		
4. Are you afraid to admit you are beginning to dislike your ill/disabled loved one?		
5. Do you sometimes drink too much alcohol, or misuse other substances?		
6. Have most of your friends disappeared since you have become a caregiver?		
7. Do you find yourself more frequently depressed or in a bad mood these days?		
8. Have you discovered that you no longer have much to talk about with your care recipient?		
9. Do you have a lot more headaches or other aches and pains lately?		
10. Are you continuing to be a caregiver because you did not grasp the full implication of your vows or promises?		
11. When you pay attention to your own needs, do you feel guilty?		
12. Do you have fantasies about having an affair?		
13. Are you neglecting the care recipient's personal hygiene?		
14. Do you sometimes yell at your ill/disabled loved one?		
15. Do you notice that your ill/disabled loved one has become indifferent to your comfort?		

Key

0-5: Your tipping point may be closer than you think.

6-10: You should be talking with someone about a Plan B.

11-15: You have already reached your tipping point—
immediate action and change is recommended.

After you have taken the Tipping Point Assessment, you may be asking yourself, "How do I get the kind of help I need if I want to survive my caregiving role?"

The next section was prepared to help you evaluate and choose significant caregiving resources that are currently available.

———

CAREGIVING HELP

Whether or not you have reached your tipping point, this section of the Guide is a practical roadmap for how to choose caregiving help and support.

Most male caregivers start this process by asking people they know—family and friends—if they can help in some way with their loved one. Let us start here.

How to "Vet" Your Caregiving Help

Finding alternative caregiving help, or locating a competent sitter so that the care recipient is never alone, can be a daunting task. The easier path is to acquire the services of a licensed and insured home health agency, but that can be expensive (we will deal with hiring below). Insurance companies and other payers usually have limits on what services are covered, and benefits eventually run out. Covered services normally require doctors' orders for a skilled service—wound care, certain therapies, urinary catheters, IV medications, etc. Home health orders frequently require caregiver training so the responsibility can be transferred to the caregiver as soon as is practical. The real hurdles are how to find reliable and reasonably priced long-term help.

The first resource male caregivers turn to is likely to be friends and family. Take the time to think carefully about your friends, relatives, and neighbors. Are there any who can be approached to support your caregiving responsibilities? If so, how can their time be scheduled so that they do not become worn out and resentful of donating their time to your ill or disabled loved one?

At the beginning of an illness, there is often an outpouring of offers for help. If you are not prepared to answer the question, "How can I help you?", let the person offering assistance know that you will cash in the rain check when the need arises.

Have these people offered help in the past? If so, take them up on the offer. Do not assume that the offers of help are simply empty social niceties. Much of what they can provide can be free.

From this point forward, when someone asks, "What can I do?", be prepared to tell them. Have a Wish List ready to go and tell them what you need.

Wish List Items for Volunteers
♦ Cook a meal once a week, once a month, etc.
♦ Gift certificates for meals that can be picked up and brought home
♦ Donations of medical equipment from garage sales or purchased new
♦ Lawn care
♦ Home maintenance chores that have been on the back burner
♦ Gasoline gift cards
♦ Sitting services
♦ Take the care recipient on a regular outing
♦ Barber or beauty salon services for the caregiver and/or the care recipient
♦ Full body massages for the caregiver as a respite treat
♦ Babysitting services for the caregiver's minor children
♦ Pay a bill, a co-pay, a utility expense

Have a Caregiver Celebration
Throw a party (or have a friend do so) similar to a housewarming—of sorts. Caregiver celebrations can assist individuals in transitioning smoothly, and with adequate supplies, into a new lifestyle due to a life-altering event.

Becoming a caregiver certainly qualifies as a life-altering event, and it often occurs without any warning. Many people are thrust into the role of caregiver without preparation, or they scramble before the loved one is discharged from the hospital.

Since individuals cannot run from the obligation, putting a positive spin on the situation can be beneficial. Have a party, and create a list of items that you and the care recipient need to make living more comfortable. For many, simply surviving the incident or illness will be a reason to celebrate. Capture the goodwill of friends and family by seeking donations via the celebration.

Gift Ideas (depending on disability)
- Grab bars
- Shower chair
- Shampoo basin
- Positioning devices (available through medical equipment suppliers)
- Incontinence supplies
- Hand-held shower head
- Toiletries
- Bed and bath supplies
- Transfer devices for safety (i.e., gait belts, walkers, lightweight wheelchairs)
- Raised toilet seat
- Adaptive eating utensils
- Adaptive devices to assist with care recipient independence
- Linens for bed and bath (caregiving requires multiple changes)

We know a man who started his own non-profit corporation because his wife had MS. He found that as the disease progressed, he could not afford to buy everything his wife needed, nor were there readily available financial resources. But due to the non-profit status of his wife's "charity," businesses, medical suppliers, and individuals were willing to donate to his non-profit.

Donors were generous. For equipment he did not need for his wife, he found other families who needed the equipment or financial aid. His only rule was that when the equipment had served its purpose, they had to return it to him so that he could continue the mission of the non-profit corporation. He received amazingly expensive items such as Hoyer lifts, pool lifts, power chairs, etc. His wife has subsequently died, but he continues the program.

Hiring or Contracting for Professional Services

Choosing caregiving help for yourself is one of the most important decisions you will make. We strongly urge you to take your time in the selection process. Stay focused on the qualities you require and do not confuse friendliness with competence and reliability.

The very first step in hiring additional help or contracting for services is to see if the potential vendor shares the core values held by you and your care recipient. This is different from buying medical equipment or supplies. But if you are going to have someone help care for someone you love, do not be afraid to ask them tough questions about their values or the values of their company. Some of these questions might include:

- How long have you provided professional caregiving services?
- What are some names of people you worked with so I can check your references?
- What are you most proud of in your history of working with caregivers?
- We all have strengths and weaknesses in everything we do. What are your strengths and weaknesses as a caregiver professional?
- How did you happen to get into this line of work?
- Have you been a caregiver for a sick or disabled loved one? What was that experience like?
- What kind of training, if any, have you had in caring for someone with chronic illness or disability?
- Will you agree to a background check?

We urge you to evaluate the personal style of the person or company you hire to help you. Some of you may not have a choice because of the limited resources that are available, but even in those cases, by asking these kinds of questions, you are putting the potential helper on notice that you deeply value the person for whom you are caring.

As a caregiver, you become the CEO of your own caregiving business. The management of your loved ones' care can require the same level of attention as a business enterprise. Caregivers must hire and fire help, manage financial resources, and allocate time to the job. If you hire an individual, we suggest you take the person on as an independent contractor. This makes them responsible for their own taxes and benefits.

Benefits in Hiring Individuals

♦ This option may be less expensive than going through an agency.

♦ Individuals are free of corporate rules and can enter into a relationship that is tailored completely to the requirements of the family.

Concerns in Hiring Individuals

♦ You have no recourse if the relationship with the paid help goes badly. You will be responsible for severing the ties safely and properly.

♦ Many people who take these jobs are notoriously cash-hungry, and often ask for cash advances, reimbursement for gasoline, and so forth. Be prepared to put your agreement in writing and be firm.

♦ A small percentage of those who work in others' homes are inclined to steal from their employer. Pay close attention to their former employers' words and tone. Their slightest hesitation in endorsing the candidate is very meaningful. Even with a good recommendation, lock up tempting valuables such as jewelry and cash.

Considerations in Hiring a Company

♦ Ask the same type of questions for hiring an individual regarding references and whether or not the employees are screened through background checks.

♦ You should also ask about the type of training, if any, the employees have pertaining to the illness, or disability, of your loved one.

Benefits in Working With a Company
+ If something goes awry with the service or personnel in your home, you have the option of calling the company that provides the service to intervene on your behalf.
+ It is likely that a company is insured and follows a regulated record-keeping protocol.

Concerns in Working With a Company
+ Services may be more expensive.
+ There may be inconsistency with personnel, including not having staff when you are depending on them.
+ There may be company rules limiting the flexibility of the personnel.

Obtaining Access to Medical Equipment

When an individual qualifies for medical equipment via a doctor's order, it is relatively easy to find a provider. The doctor will likely have a relationship with a home health agency or medical equipment provider that he or she recommends.

It is important to realize that you can find your own providers. You are not obligated to use organizations associated with your medical providers. The caregiver is in charge and always has the option of interviewing sales reps for each company and establishing a relationship.

Be Pro-Active and Be Prepared

You are the primary caregiver and you need to be ready to do the job. Male caregivers must take command of the environment and the situation. That includes doctor appointments and home health visits. Medical and even caregiving professionals will not presume to know what is going on in the caregiver's home. You must be prepared to advocate for your own needs by laying out all of the pertinent experiences in a short amount of time. In general, professionals have only about fifteen minutes to complete an assessment before they move on to another patient. Caregivers need to prepare an efficient presentation for the professional in order to make the most of their allotted time.

Faith-Based Resources

Faith-based resources can be a real caregiving asset and strength. Some men rely on their faith and their faith community for sustenance and support during caregiving. Men often believe that caring for their loved one entails a spiritual mission that exceeds merely dressing a wound, preparing a meal, or cleaning a bedpan. Men have commented on how their own faith and spirituality have been both tested and strengthened during caregiving. Some have said it was only their deep spiritual beliefs that held them up, even after their loved one died. It is important for us to recognize that for spiritually oriented men, their faith is a real strength.

Many faith-based organizations also provide concrete assistance to informal caregivers in a variety of ways as part of their larger mission. Importantly, most of these programs are normally open to caregivers of any faith: a caregiver does not need to be a member of the congregation from which the assistance comes. Some of the programs and services include:

- ♦ Respite rooms
- ♦ Errand running
- ♦ Food pantry—particularly helpful during the holidays
- ♦ Adult sitting services (i.e., companionship for the ill person)
- ♦ Recreational outlets inside the home (card games like bridge, bunko, etc.)
- ♦ Spiritual counseling for informal caregivers
- ♦ Mental health services via licensed professionals available on a sliding scale
- ♦ Caregiver support groups; frequently the available support groups are not affiliated with the religious organization but borrow or rent their space

Many caregivers have shared their stories about faith-based assistance. Here are a few examples:

A husband and father, caring for his wife, was struggling to manage holiday stress. A friend anonymously contacted a faith-based organization and requested that this family receive a holiday meal to alleviate the stress, not because the man could not afford to feed his family, but because he was overwhelmed with responsibilities. The gift was deeply appreciated and meaningful to the family; they were able to enjoy the holiday as a family without the added pressure of cooking.

—

A son used a church's outreach program to provide his mother with much needed social contact since she could not leave her home due to the multiple pieces of medical equipment. They had a standing appointment for bridge games in her home and he was able to relax, knowing his mom was happily occupied when he was at work.

—

A man caring for his wife diagnosed with Alzheimer's disease was able to sign up for the local Catholic charity respite program. This enabled him to drop her off at the church for a few hours every Thursday afternoon. He gratefully acknowledged that this respite helped him remained "sane."

—

Bill's mother was physically handicapped with multiple ailments. She had a lot of trouble accepting her limitations and put enormous pressure on Bill to transport her everywhere, limiting his ability to focus on his small business. A local Methodist church offered low cost psychological counseling services provided by several of the parishioners. Bill persuaded his mother to attend group counseling sessions at the church. Bill later reported that his mother cut back on her demands and he was able to give his business the required attention.

—

We hope this information helps you to find and ask for assistance from your faith community if you need it. Many faith-based leaders report that men are more reluctant to ask and they want to see more men come forward.

———

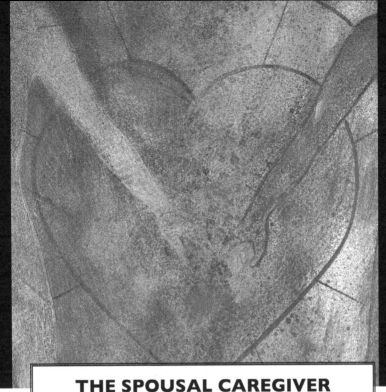

THE SPOUSAL CAREGIVER

What makes spousal caregiving so unique is that finances and sexual intimacy are automatically involved. Some of us contribute to an ill parent's well-being, or we monitor our disabled sibling's affairs, but when our spouse is ill, we lose an important part of our own life along the way. In non-spousal caregiving situations, our spouse is usually by our side in delivering care and sharing our experiences equally.

There is no caregiver role quite as complex and emotionally draining as caring for a spouse. Until a person fully acknowledges that the role is emotionally complex and often painful and isolating, it is almost impossible to plan and reclaim some sense of normalcy. What we have found is that spousal caregivers frequently do not admit that they are "caregivers" for several years because they believe they are simply doing their duty according to promises and wedding vows. However, honoring the vows takes on a whole new meaning when delivering care consumes the entire marital relationship and the ill partner's needs get all the attention.

Some of us are not legally married to our life partner, but with or without traditional wedding vows, we made promises to care for them. We may love them deeply and believe that this role of caregiver is our obligation, regardless of the personal sacrifices it entails. It is commonly accepted that we refer to this role as the spousal caregiver, with or without a wedding. We use that terminology here because it is much easier to locate additional information and talk to professionals using this common term.

Most self-help resources do not address the two unique characteristics of spousal caregiving—sex and money— because of certain obstacles. First, spousal caregivers feel a sense of disloyalty when they self-identify as a caregiver instead of a spouse. Most spousal caregivers can recall a point where they suddenly realized they were no longer living as a husband but as an errand runner, nursing assistant, driver, etc.

Secondly, the healthy spouse knows that many family members and friends will not understand what living like a caregiver really means because marriages and intimate relationships are inherently private matters. Other possibilities are that well, healthy spousal caregivers are sometimes scolded for confiding their feelings to others. Many have been exposed so frequently to the previously mentioned caregiver myths that they begin to distrust their own judgment.

To make all of this more difficult, health care professionals sometimes ignore the issues in a marriage dealing with chronic disability. Society, plus family and friends, will often dictate expectations about the healthy spouse's behavior without asking what he wants or needs to survive the situation.

The plight of the male spousal caregiver is frequently misunderstood. Our friends never ask how our marriage is holding up through the medical bills; that would be socially unacceptable. Consequently, the spousal caregiver lives in emotional isolation. Our partner's doctor never asks how our sex life is because he or she does not want to address an emotionally volatile subject. As a result, the spousal caregiver stays quiet about the loneliness and celibacy. Our ill spouse never mentions that she misses the old life because it causes too much pain emotionally, and possibly physically. The healthy spouse refrains from honest discussions about the bills and the rejection he feels. In turn, all of these actions can make the spousal caregiver more isolated and angry than is necessary.

Sex and Spousal Caregiving

We get married for companionship and sexual intimacy. It is important to acknowledge that marriages and intimate relationships are partnerships. When illness or disability strike, it is not wrong to sometimes feel cheated, lonely, and as if you are not cared for any longer by your partner. These are normal reactions.

What happens to intimacy? Caregiving can destroy desire for our life partner, but there are often times when the opposite is true. Desire is often there for both partners, but the caregivers may be afraid to act. He does not want to hurt his partner or start something he cannot finish. One complication may be that medical equipment "gets in the way."

Male caregivers often believe it is wrong to act on sexual desires due to the partner's illness. Many men whose wives have dementia-related illnesses say that they feel intimacy with her does not feel consensual, and therefore they abstain. The problem is that the wives report that they feel abandoned sexually. Each man will have to discuss this with his wife and address these issues. Some illnesses do not move at rapid rates and there is plenty of time to capture every good moment.

Still, many men look for cues from their partner to initiate moments of intimacy. They spend their time waiting, waiting, and waiting. What some men do not understand is that their ill partner is feeling fear. She fears that she is undesirable now and is scared that there are limitations. But the couple may not have been candid with their health care providers and *asked* if there are any limitations.

Sexuality is private; few people talk about in caregiving support groups. Yet, it is a topic spousal caregivers yearn to discuss with others who are in the same boat. Most caregivers hope that doctors will initiate the sexual intimacy discussion, but research indicates that most will not because they do not feel comfortable with the subject. However, they will discuss it when prompted by the patient. Caregivers need to feel empowered to ask the tough questions about sex.

The nature of the marital/life partner relationship prior to the illness or disability may need to be examined. The prior relationship could impact the desire to deliver care in a supportive fashion. Or it could impede communication if the relationship was strained. . Professionals state that behaviors and actions that were present in a relationship prior to caregiving often are amplified–things do not get better just because someone is sick—that is another myth.

So what's a man to do?

♦ Use open communication to construct a new relationship, given the new limitations. This may be difficult, but insist because this will help both of you live a more meaningful life.

♦ Initiate creativity, assuming that both of you are interested in establishing some physical contact. Examples include maintaining one room for care delivery and another for marital intimacy so that the intimacy room is free of images and memories of caregiving procedures.

♦ Minimize fears. You may be afraid of something unnecessarily. Talk to a health care professional about any limitations. If you do not get a satisfactory answer, seek other opinions.

Finances and Spousal Caregiving

Both the caregiver and the wife are living out of the same pool of resources. If both have been working and the ill spouse suddenly no longer contributes to the household finances, it places more pressure on the working spouse. He can no longer afford a day off, and the financial stability of the family is on his shoulders. This can be especially difficult when there is inadequate savings, limited health insurance, and the couple has been living paycheck to paycheck.

More significantly, the working, healthy spouse is also likely providing care to the ill spouse when the workday is through. Therefore, he gets little chance for rest and recuperation. On the chance that care is not being provided by the healthy spouse, finances remain tight because medical needs, insurance co-payments, medicines, and medical equipment are eating up whatever money is available. The spousal caregiver might well feel resentful of the fact that he is working hard, barely scraping by, and seeing no personal reward for all of his diligence. As we discussed in the caregiver mythology section, it is not wrong to think of yourself, because both caregiver and recipient need to find ways to survive the health setback.

———

A Note on Caring for Parents

Often the financial resources of a married couple are used for the care of one set of disabled or ill parents. Often the potential inheritance of a child has to be redirected to the cost of care for the parents. The decision about how to use the parent's resources can limit the adult child's financial willingness to help.

Living arrangements in such a situation can be costly, both emotionally and financially. This is a big issue; there are different dynamics between parents moving in for care (parents have to become subordinates because the man is king of his castle) and children caring for the parents at their parents' home (he reverts to the child role). There are subtle issues pertaining to power. Regardless of the depth of relationship dynamics, these complications come into play, and the caregiving man must be prepared.

Other factors include the role of other family members. In extended families, sibling relationships, step-siblings, step-parents, half siblings, and so forth, often make for a complicated picture. Where are all those people now? Many emotions are involved in evaluating who is available and seeking support. There can also be issues of jealousy depending on who steps forward to take some responsibility.

We urge you to read a ground-breaking book on spousal caregiving by Dave and Rhonda Travland called *The Tough & Tender Caregiver: A Handbook for the Well Spouse.*

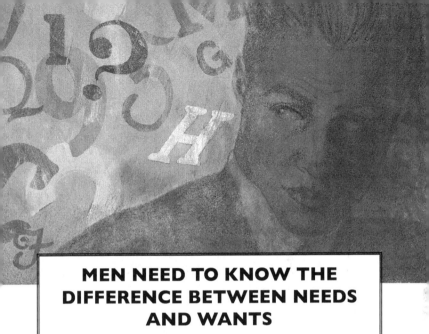

MEN NEED TO KNOW THE DIFFERENCE BETWEEN NEEDS AND WANTS

As discussed earlier in the mythology section, men sometimes believe that the needs of the care recipient are more important than their own needs. The truth, of course, is that everybody's needs are important. The needs of the care recipient, however, are frequently more visible and obvious. These needs are more prominent because of the physical limitations and the emotional distress that illness can bring. Compassion takes over and caregivers work continually to meet those demands. However, that does not mean those needs are more *important* than the needs of the caregiver.

A caregiving man needs to commit this very important principle to memory: If the needs of the caregiver are not met, the caregiver cannot continue to give care. The danger is that the quality of the care he delivers will deteriorate if he does not follow the principle. Ignoring self-needs means that everyone loses. Caregiver needs must be a priority, right next to quality care.

Looking at the difference between needs and wants, we can immediately see that there is something dysfunctional about treating needs and wants in the same category. In theory, needs are fundamental to well-being and wants tend to be whimsical, superficial, or short-term in nature. People will suffer if their needs are not met, but they will not suffer if their wants are not met.

In caregiving, the line is blurred between needs and wants for several reasons. First, because care recipients are often deprived of a normal life due to their limitations, they ask for wants to be filled as if they were needs. They feel like they should be compensated for the limitations and may take that compensation in the form of a kind of caregiver servitude. They often fall into the pattern of demanding services from the caregiver. For a man, this is a vulnerable spot, especially when the care recipient is female (wife or mother); chivalry and respect for the fairer sex supersedes his own desire to limit the serving of wants.

Secondly, it is necessary to meet the needs of *both* the caregiver and the care recipient before anyone's wants are met. As stated, needs are necessary and wants are less important. However, in caregiving, wants are essential to mental health for both parties. A caregiver knows all too well that he makes sacrifices regularly. Determining what his wants are is also critical. Does he want to play golf?

Does he want to go have a drink with friends? Has he excised those activities from his life and found himself angry? If the answer is yes, then some of the wants must be acknowledged and met so that the anger does not translate into neglect or abuse.

In order to carve out time for respite, the male caregiver must make a distinction between what the care recipient needs versus what he or she merely wants. The key component is mastering the art of saying no, meaning it, and making it into a new habit. Caregivers need to understand that it is safe to say no to wants, but it is not always safe to say no to needs.

The truth is that saying no is a lifeline for a caregiver. Knowing when you are able to say no, having the willingness to say no, and never saying yes out of guilt is a survival tactic.

———

THE "IDEAL" BALANCED MALE CAREGIVER

The balanced caregiving man:

♦ Is flexible—he can handle any problems because he can mentally leap into a new challenge

- Is a good problem solver
- Maintains his own social network away from the care recipient
- Trusts his instincts
- Allows emotions to surface rather than avoiding or suppressing them
- Appreciates both efficiency and innovation
- Properly cares for his own needs with equal importance to the care recipient's

The Balanced Caregiver is firmly in touch with reality, understands himself, his environment, and how to make himself comfortable in his caregiving environment. The Balanced Caregiver knows what he needs and how to get those needs met. Because conditions change, the Balanced Caregivers realizes he must be open to new learning in order to stay in touch with reality. He is always prepared to give up what he believes if it is not working and substitute something that will work. With tough-minded intentions, the outcomes of the Balanced Caregiver's decisions meet his needs while providing care for his loved one.

These men understand that they must take the right kind of action in order to get their needs met. If they are successful, they will be happy. However, a word of caution: nobody is or can be a Balanced Caregiver all the time. Even if you are most of the time, it really takes effort. Even when things turn out well, getting there may not have been pretty. There will be false starts, mid-course corrections, and the need to back up and re-think strategy. The Balanced Caregiver can come from any generation. In the following ideal caregiver profile, the male caregiver is very flexible and can move with ease in response to situational demands. He is a protector with compassion.

He is comfortable with himself, knows and lives out his core values, but he also appreciates and enjoys his own social network. He listens to advice, but also trusts his instincts. He reacts with anger when appropriate but he does not fly off the handle. He appreciates efficiency and innovation to create the best possible life for both himself and his care recipient. He manages his responsibilities properly and cares for his own needs.

How the Balanced Caregiver Faces the Challenges Most Male Caregivers Face

Typical challenges	How it is managed
Deliver care and still work	Sets and maintains a strict schedule.
Needs personal down time	He sleeps and rests when the care recipient is resting. He does not try to accomplish unfinished business at that time.
May have no one to lean on	He maintains his relationships with friends, including women, because those friendships bolster his masculinity and self-worth when he is feeling defeated and vulnerable.
Sexual intimacy is compromised	He is honest with his partner and encourages open discussions so that intimacy does not suffer. (Suggestions: medical supply companies have equipment to assist based on limitations, web sites supporting couples managing spinal cord injuries have a wealth of information and suggestions that apply to a variety of disabilities.)
Care recipient's wants are consuming	He knows the power of the word "no" and recognizes that he cannot cater to every request because to do so compromises his well-being. He routinely reminds his loved one that he must take care of himself, or they both lose.

Below, we have constructed a "Day in the Life of a Balanced Male Caregiver" based on some of the best caregiving practices we have witnessed.

George has created an agenda that insures that Emily's needs are met along with his own.

A Day in the Life of a Balanced Caregiver – Spouse

Morning Chores
George awakens to the sunlight streaming in his bedroom window at 6 A.M. He immediately begins his usual morning routine.

♦ He kisses Emily awake, asks her how she slept, and helps her into her wheelchair for her morning trip to the bathroom.

♦ He helps her onto the commode and leaves; he then changes her bed.

♦ When Emily is finished, he cleans her up, helps her dress, and assists her back into the wheelchair.

♦ George then wheels her to the kitchen, brings her the morning paper, and begins preparing breakfast.

♦ While they eat breakfast he explains the details of the day to her—that he will be at work beginning at 9 A.M.

but that he will be home for lunch, as usual. He asks
her where she would like to be left during that three-
hour period. She chooses to sit at the computer for
the balance of the morning.

♦ George wheels her to the computer, brings her
something to drink and snack on, kisses her goodbye,
and leaves for work.

Noon Activities

George arrives home at 12:15 P.M., checks on Emily, who
is dozing in her wheelchair, and begins lunch
preparations.

♦ When lunch is ready he wheels Emily to the
bathroom and waits for her to finish.

♦ Back in the kitchen, she describes her morning online
activities while they eat lunch, and he shares some
stories about customers at work.

♦ Emily begins to complain about pain, and George
retrieves her pain medication for her.

♦ Emily begs George not to return to work, but he
patiently explains that he has no choice but to return.

♦ George changes the subject to what Emily would like
to do this afternoon, and she names two books she
would like to read in the sun room. George arranges
this and returns to work.

Dinner Time

When George returns home at 5:30 P.M., Emily is again
fast asleep in her chair. George lets her sleep, has a cup of
coffee while reading the paper, and takes about an hour's

nap. He realizes that Emily will be up a portion of the night, so he sleeps when he can.

♦ Emily wakes him announcing she is hungry.
♦ George wheels Emily to the bathroom, then goes to the kitchen to begin dinner preparations.
♦ He cleans her up, puts medication on some skin abrasions, helps her back into the wheelchair, and takes her to the kitchen for dinner.
♦ George listens to Emily's complaints for about ten minutes, reassures her that he will do what he can to make her comfortable, and shares some of his work stories from that afternoon.
♦ George explains that he needs to leave the house again after dinner to shop for groceries, and they work out an activity for her for when he is out.

Evening Activities

When George returns from the grocery store, he puts everything away and puts Emily in front of the TV in the living room.

♦ Together they watch two consecutive programs they both enjoy.
♦ They discuss the day's activities. George makes an effort to keep Emily informed of current events that interest her. He reviews information about family and friends.
♦ He inquires if she has any expectations for activities the next day and determines whether (and how) he can meet those expectations.

- He offers Emily a favorite dessert and they laugh about how long she has loved this specific treat.
- At 11 P.M. George sits next to Emily and asks her how she feels about physical intimacy that evening. She beams at him and he wheels her into the bedroom.
- He quickly assembles the medical sexual aids that allow them to have sex without causing Emily any discomfort. She watches him work with a silly grin on her face until he helps her into his bed.
- Afterwards, he helps her get comfortable in her own bed, kisses her good night, and begins reading himself to sleep.
- At 2 A.M. Emily suddenly awakens from a bad dream. George fixes her a cup of cocoa and a cookie, talks with her for thirty minutes, and she falls asleep again.
- George returns to bed and sleeps until morning.

———

A FINAL WORD

We hope that men will take our ideal model as a challenge. We truly believe the closer you can come to being healthy, balanced, and guilt free, the better caregiver you will be. Our Balanced Caregiver is always in the catbird seat, equipped with the flexibility that will be so very useful over the long haul in any caregiving situation. We all need to strive to be a balanced, healthy, and guilt-free caregiver.

"Care is a state in which something does matter; it is the source of human tenderness." – Rollo May

You are unique—but one powerful thread weaves though all male caregivers: the love they have for the person they care for.

You are just as committed and emotionally involved with caregiving as women; you just express yourself differently. If men seem to manage care, be too protective, not shed many tears, look for ways to be economical without sacrificing quality, and not talk much about their feelings, we should not be surprised. For men, these qualities are viewed by society as male strengths. Men do not back down from a challenge and they are not afraid to fight for what might seem to be impossible outcomes.

As we have seen throughout this Guide, caregiving can also be very confusing for men. It can depress them, make them feel selfish, even make them question the depth of their love.

Erich Fromm wrote a great deal about what authentic love is and what it really means. He says the true nature of love has the common elements of care, responsibility, respect, and knowledge (of what other people truly want and need). He also said love is a union with somebody outside oneself, under the condition of keeping our own separateness and the integrity of our own self.

In other words, if you are not able to truly feel love for yourself and maintain your own integrity as a caregiver, you will never be able to love the person you are caring for in the most complete way. You never want to say, "I love you because I need you." Instead you want to say, "I need you because I love you."

We only hope this Guide has pointed you in directions that will help you find some of the right caregiving answers for yourself.

– Jim and Rhonda

———

~APPENDIX~
TARGETED RESOURCES
FOR MALE CAREGIVERS

As we prepared this Appendix, we were aware that in this digital age, many resources come and go without warning. So in vetting these resources, we used the following referral criteria:

- ◆ The resource has existed for more than five years
- ◆ The resource is found nationally, but not necessarily in every state
- ◆ The resource can help you find other related resources
- ◆ The resource does not discriminate based on race, age, religion, or national origin or disability

(Some websites below change without notice. If this happens, we apologize in advance.)

A. National Caregiver Organizations
www.caregiver.com
This is perhaps the best and most complete resource available; we urge men to start their search for additional help here.

The Family Caregiver Alliance
www.nfcacares.org
The lead agency in California's system of Caregiver Resource Centers, the FCA operates the National Center on Caregiving to advance the development of support programs for family caregivers in every state.

www.wellspouse.org
You will find resources here exclusively dedicated to the spousal caregiver.

www.nhpco.org

This the site for the National Hospice and Palliative Care Organization. They have a resource site that can be accessed through **www.caringinfo.org** which includes additional palliative caregiving resources.

www.archrespite.org
www.respitelocator.org

The mission of the ARCH National Respite Network and Resource Center is to assist and promote the development of quality respite and crisis care programs; to help families locate respite and crisis care services in their communities; and to serve as a strong voice for respite in all forums.

Shepherd's Centers of America (SCA)
www.shepherdcenters.org

An interfaith, not-for-profit organization that coordinates nearly 100 independent Shepherd's Centers across the US to help older adults remain independent in their own living situation.

The Center for Family Caregivers
www.caregiving.com
www.familycaregivers.org

The Center for Family Caregivers and Denise Brown operate Tad Publishing Co., which produces books, newsletters, and other materials for families and health care professionals who care for chronically ill or disabled family members.

The Caregivers Advisory Panel
www.caregiversadvisorypanel.com

Collects confidential information on the opinions and needs of family caregivers to help health care product manufacturers and service providers to create innovative products, services, programs, and support for America's caregiving families.

www.caringroad.com

CaringRoad.com is dedicated to helping family caregivers obtain information, locate services, and find support so that they can make informed decisions about the care of their loved ones.

www.n4a.org

The National Association of Area Agencies on Aging's primary mission is to build the capacity of its members to help older people and people with disabilities live with dignity and choices in their homes and communities for as long as possible. Enter this link to see an example of what you can receive from a local Area Agency on Aging: **www.app.e2ma.net/app/view:CampaignPublic/id:18978.88 03997624/rid:914ba663371544ce991bd8716521c71f**

www.aarp.org

The American Associations of Retired Persons offers various articles and other resources on caregiving.

www.4woman.gov

The National Women's Health Information Center has information on caregiver stress.

B. National Organizations for Specific Acute or Chronic Conditions

There are many local affiliates of these national organizations that produce very good materials that you can access online. Our advice is to first go to the national website and see what they offer; in most cases these websites will identify branches or chapters in your state.

Here are the resources we have found most helpful:

www.alz.org

www.dementiacaregiving101.com

www.ehow.com/dementia-caregiver

www.alsa.org

www.mdausa.org/publications/alscare

www.diabetes.org

www.parkinsons.org

www.cancer.gov

www.cancer.org

www.hdsa.org

www.ascaa.org

www.arthritis.org

www.epilepsyfoundation.org

www.heart.org/heartorg

www.apparelyzed.com

www.paralysis.org/Caregivers/CaregiversMain.cfm

Spinal Cord Injury Caregivers
www.groups.yahoo.com/group/scic
Yahoo Internet Forum is a place to share information and to support other caregivers who are caring for people with SCI.

www.muhealth.org/~momscis/manual.htm
Missouri Model Spinal Cord Injury System's Enhancing Independence: A Personal Attendant Training Manual (pdf file). Downloadable and free.

www.spinalcord.org
NSCIA website section on caregiving.

C. Securing Outside Help

If you are looking for outside help, listed here are groups that exist specifically for caregivers. Because we have found the quality of care provided by these groups to differ by state and locality, we urge you, for your own protection, to use the vetting process we presented in this Guide. At a minimum, check with the Better Business Bureau (to see if complaints have been filed against any potential providers), your local Area Agency on Aging, your state agencies that handle Medicare and Medicaid, and your state insurance commission or the body that regulates insurance companies in your state.

www.carewatchers.org

www.comfortkeepers.com

www.strengthforcaring.com

www.visitingangels.com

www.tbi-sci.org/pdf/pas.pdf

Hiring and Management of Personal Care Assistants for Individuals with SCI. A downloadable 26-page booklet from the SCI Project at Santa Clara Valley Medical Center. Covers everything from locating and hiring to training personal assistants. Includes forms, checklists and resources. (In pdf format.)

PCA Guide
www.wa-ilsc.org/toc2ack.html

Online guide to managing attendants from the Washington Coalition of Citizens with disABILITIES, the Independent Living Service Center in Everett, WA, and the Disability Resource Network in Redmond, WA.

D. Digital Tools

Here are some new digital tools that might be helpful:

www.care-profiler.com

www.DrMarion.com

E. Caregiving Newsletters

Take Care! A quarterly newsletter from the National Family Caregivers Association. Subscribe at: **www.nfcacares.org**

Today's Caregiver. Published six times a year by Caregiver Media Group. Subscribe at **www.caregiver.com**

Online Newsletters

Caregiver.com Free newsletter sent once a week via email. Subscribe at **www.caregiver.com**

Family Caregiver Alliance Update. Free newsletter readable at **www.caregiver.org newsletter.html**
Also see their Fact Sheets, readable online.

F. Selected Books on Caregiving

Here is a list of books we have found helpful. We also urge you to check Amazon.com and other electronic book sources to find the latest publications. An excellent guide to find e-books is:
www.lifehack.org/articles/technology/a-beginners-guide-to-e-books.html

Barg, Gary. *The Fearless Caregiver: How to Get the Best Care for Your Loved One and Still Have a Life of Your Own.* Sterling, VA: Capital Books, 2001.

DeGraff, Alfred H. *Caregivers and Personal Assistants: How to Find, Hire and Manage the People Who Help You (Or Your Loved One!).* 3rd ed. Fort Collins, CO: Saratoga Access Publications Inc., 2002.

Drattell, Alan. *The Other Victim: How Caregivers Survive a Loved One's Chronic Illness.* Santa Ana, CA: Seven Locks Press, 1996. (Multiple sclerosis caregivers' stories.)

Holicky, Richard. *Taking Care of Yourself While Providing Care: A Guide for Those Who Assist and Care for Their Spouses, Children, Parents, and Other Loved Ones Who Have Spinal Cord Injuries.* Englewood, CO: Craig Hospital, 2000. (Call 303-789-8202 to order for $5.00.)

Ilardo, Joseph and Carole R. Rothman. *I'll Take Care of You: A Practical Guide for Family Caregivers.* Oakland, CA: New Harbinger Publications, 1999.

Meyer, Maria M. and Paula Derr. *The Comfort of Home: An Illustrated Step-by-Step Guide for Caregivers.* Portland, OR: CareTrust Publications, 1998.

Nieboer, Laura. *Home Care Organizer For Families Providing Home Care.* Washington, DC: State of the Art, Inc., 1997.

Thompson, Gretchen. *God Knows Caregiving Can Pull You Apart: 12 Ways to Keep It All Together.* Notre Dame, IN: Sorin Books, 2002.

Travland, David and Rhonda Travland. *The Tough & Tender Caregiver: A Handbook for the Well Spouse.* Booksurge, 2009.

About the Authors

James V. Gambone, Ph.D., is an Adjunct Professor of Gerontology in the Graduate School of Public Service Leadership at Capella University. Jim is also one of the country's leading authorities and generational and intergenerational relationships. He is a published author, motivational speaker, and consultant. He was also a caregiving helper for his grandmother at a young age and has personally supported other men in chronic and acute caregiving situations.

Besides being a leader in the field of aging, Jim is an award-winning film and television writer, producer, and director. His latest film, *The Journey Home* deals with the future of elder care in the U.S. and Jim's newest book, *ReFirement: A Guide To Midlife and Beyond* has been well received by Boomers across the country. It asks the important question to America's largest generation: "What will you do with the third act of your life?"

Rhonda Travland, M.S., is a gerontologist, social worker, author, and educator. She is currently working on her Ph.D. in Human Services. She was a caregiver to her husband for 17 years. He was a victim of Young Onset Alzheimer's Disease. Her experience as a spousal caregiver gives her unique insight into the stress and frustration of caring for a chronically ill loved one. She is uniquely qualified to help caregivers develop practical strategies for surviving the stress of the caregiving situation.

Her background includes over a decade as a licensed nursing home administrator, serving as CEO of a service business, and serving as a professional consultant to private industry in corporate America. She is president of the Caregiver Survival Institute.

———

Made in the USA
Charleston, SC
23 March 2012